The Little Pink Pig

by Liza Charlesworth
illustrated by Doug Jones

SCHOLASTIC INC.

New York • Toronto • London • Auckland • Sydney
Mexico City • New Delhi • Hong Kong • Buenos Aires

Designed by Maria Lilja
ISBN-13: 978-0-439-88453-2 • ISBN-10: 0-439-88453-5
Copyright © 2006 by Scholastic Inc.
All rights reserved. Printed in China.

First printing, September 2006

12 11 10 9 8 7 6 5 4   7 8 9 10 11/0

Once upon a time, there **lived** a **little pink pig**. Her name was **Kim**.

Kim **did** not like being **little** or **pink**. And she really **did** not like the **dimple in** her **chin**.

One day, **Kim** met a fairy named **Jill**.
"I **will give** you **six wishes**," said Fairy **Jill**.

"**Yippee!**" said **Kim**.
She **slipped** a **wish list** from her purse.

"My first **wish is** to be **big** like a **hippo**," said **Kim**. **Zippity zip**! Fairy **Jill did it**!

"My second **wish is** to have green **skin** like a **lizard**," said **Kim**.
Zippity zip! Fairy **Jill did it**!

"My third **wish is** to have **thick** feathers like a
chicken," said **Kim**.
Zippity zip! Fairy **Jill did it**!

"My fourth **wish is** to have a **swishy** tail like a **fish**," said **Kim**.
Zippity zip! Fairy **Jill did it**!

"My **fifth wish is** to have a cute **chin** like a **chimp**," said **Kim**.
Zippity zip! Fairy **Jill did it**!

Kim looked **in** the **silver mirror**.
"**Ick**! I'm so **mixed** up," cried **Kim**. "I **think**
I **miss** the old me!"

Then **Kim** remembered! She **still** had one **wish** left to **fix** her **mistake**.

"My **sixth wish is** to be me again," said
Kim with a **grin**.
Zippity zip! Fairy **Jill did it**!

Kim was so **thrilled** to be a **little pink pig with** a **dimple in** her **chin** that she **did** a **big jig!** And **Kim** never **wished** to be **different** again.

Short-i Riddles

Listen to the riddles. Then match each riddle with the right short-*i* word from the box.

Word Box

jig	chicken	pig	wish	chimp
big	fish	grin	pink	mirror

1. This animal says, "Oink, oink!"

2. It means the opposite of *little*.

3. This bird lives on a farm and lays eggs.

4. Many pigs are this color.

5. This is another word for *monkey*.

6. You look in one to comb your hair.

7. This animal has fins and a tail.

8. This word means almost the same thing as *smile*.

9. A leprechaun does this kind of dance.

10. A fairy grants this with her magic wand.

Short-i Cheer

Hooray for short *i*, the best sound around!

Let's holler short-*i* words all over town!

There's **pig** and **trip** and **wish** and **miss**.

There's **lip** and **fish** and **drink** and **dish**.

There's **skip** and **milk** and **six** and **big**.

There's **pink** and **chimp** and **dish** and **wig**.

Short *i*, short *i*, give a great cheer,

For the most **interesting** sound you ever **will** hear!

Make a list of other short-*i* words. Then use them in your cheer.